THE FOUR BIGGEST MISTAKES IN OPTION TRADING

JAY KAEPPEL

TRADE SECRETS
The Four Biggest Mistakes
IN OPTION TRADING
JAY KAEPPEL
DIRECTOR OF RESEARCH, ESSEX TRADING COMPANY, LTD.

Published by The Traders' Library

ISBN 1-883272-22-X

Printed in the United States of America.

Contents

INTRODUCTION

Options offer traders and investors a number of outstanding opportunities. Speculators can buy options and enjoy the potential for unlimited profits with limited risk. Other traders may employ strategies that offer an extremely high probability of profit. In addition, investors can use options to hedge other existing stock or futures positions. Yet despite all of these potential benefits, it is commonly estimated that 90% of option traders lose money in the long run. This is a staggering figure that raises several extremely relevant questions:

A) What is it about option trading that causes so many people to fail?

B) Is there a way to avoid the apparently huge pitfalls that claim so many traders?

C) If the failure rate is so high, why does anybody bother trading options in the first place?

In listening to a large number of traders talk about their ideas on trading options over the years, it is interesting to note that there are several common themes running through many of these discussions. This raises an interesting question. If 90% of option traders lose money, and a lot of traders subscribe to the same ideas, can one gain an edge by avoiding the common approaches used by these traders? In order to answer this question we systematically tested the option trading approaches most commonly mentioned using computer simulations.

As we will detail in the following sections, there are several common pitfalls that the majority of option traders fall into that cause them to lose money in the long run. The good news in all of this is that by isolating these mistakes, and learning why they are so common, why they cause losses in the long run and how they can be avoided, you can make a major step toward becoming a more consistently profitable option trader.

There are good trading ideas and bad trading ideas. One of the best ways to find the good ideas is to first eliminate the bad ones. This is what we will attempt to accomplish in the following discussions where we will focus on the four biggest (and most common) mistakes made by the majority of option traders.

For each of the four biggest mistakes in option trading we will first discuss what the mistake is. We will then explain why it is so common for traders to make this mistake and why it causes traders to lose money in the long run. Finally, we will detail what needs to be done in order to avoid each mistake.

❖

One word of warning: A lot of traders may not enjoy reading these sections for the simple reason that we are about to de-bunk several ideas that many traders hold near and dear. Most often when someone attacks an idea that you believe to be true, the first reaction is to become defensive and try to defend your reasons for believing the idea in the first place. It is impossible to overemphasize the importance of reading the following text with an *open mind* if you want to trade options profitably in the long run. This is especially true given the following paradox that we have found: In most cases, the very ideas that lure traders into the options market in the first place are the same ideas that cause them to lose money in the long run.

THE FOUR BIGGEST MISTAKES IN OPTION TRADING

MISTAKE #1
Relying Solely on Market Timing To Trade Options

Why Traders Make Mistake #1

A lot of first-time option traders view options simply as a tool for leveraging their market timing decisions. That is, rather than buying or selling short a particular stock or futures contract, they feel that they can buy a call or put option and:

A) Commit a great deal less capital, and;
B) Obtain a great deal more leverage.

This is in fact possible via option trading. By putting a relatively small sum of money into an option it is possible for a trader to achieve a much higher rate of return on a given trade than if he had bought or sold short the underlying security directly. That is the good news. Unfortunately, a vast number of market timers adopt the belief that market timing is all they need to profit in options. Accordingly, they do little or no option analysis — instead adopting the attitude that "if my timing is good, any old option will do." This is a fatal error in the long run.

Market timers take great comfort in their winning trades. Any winning trades serve to reinforce their belief that market timing is all that is required to succeed, regardless of how few and far between the winning trades may be. Unfortunately, achieving a high rate of return on a given trade is NOT the same as making money in the long run. The question is not "do you achieve a big winner now and then?" Even the worst traders can occasionally hit a big winner. The relevant question is "are you following an approach that is likely to generate profits over the long run?" Traders who rely solely on market timing to trade options must answer "NO" to this all important question. The primary reason that this approach fails is that it completely ignores one of the most important factors in option trading — implied volatility. Before proceeding to explain why market timing fails option traders in the long run, let's first explain what implied volatility is and why it is so important to option trading success.

Implied Volatility Defined

The "implied volatility" value for a given option is the value that one would need to plug into an option pricing model to make the model's option price equal the current market price of an option given that the other variables (underlying price, days to expiration, interest rates and the difference between the option's strike price and the price of the underlying security) are known. In other words, it is the volatility "implied" by the current market price for a given option. For a detailed explanation of implied volatility as well as an example, please see Appendix A.

As you can see in Figures 1 and 2, the implied volatility for the options of a given security can fluctuate widely over a period of time. Also, each stock and futures market establishes its own range of highs and lows for implied volatility. Without knowing the range of volatility levels for each security it is impossible to compare apples to apples when comparing two or more underlying securities.

FIGURE 1 - IMPLIED VOLATILITY FOR INTEL OPTIONS

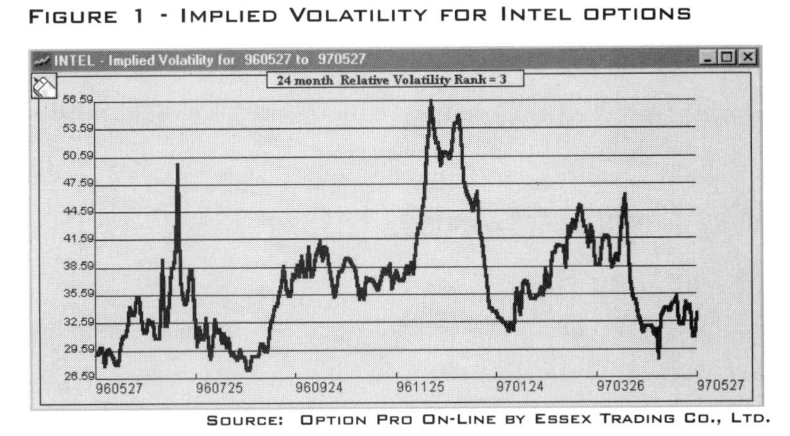

SOURCE: OPTION PRO ON-LINE BY ESSEX TRADING CO., LTD.

In Figure 1 you can see that the implied volatility for options on Intel stock has ranged from 26.69% to 56.59% with a current reading of about 33%.

FIGURE 2 - IMPLIED VOLATILITY FOR GOLD OPTIONS

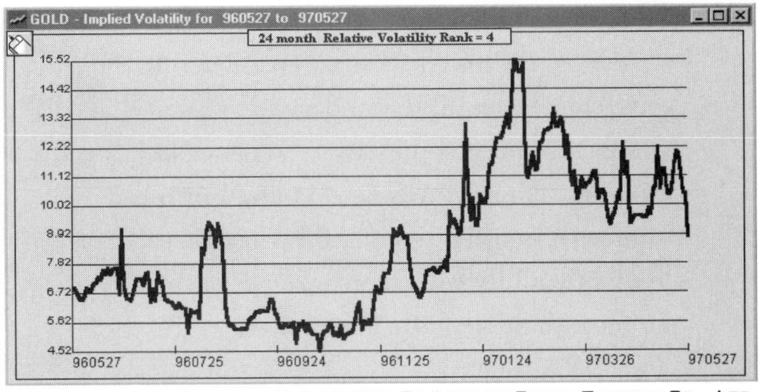

SOURCE: OPTION PRO ON-LINE BY ESSEX TRADING CO., LTD.

In Figure 2 you can see that the implied volatility for options on Gold futures has ranged from 4.52% to 15.52% with a current reading of about 8.9%.

If you simply compared the current raw values (33% to 8.9%) you would assume that volatility for Intel options is high and that volatility for Gold options is low. However, as you can see, on a relative basis the current option volatilities for both Intel and Gold are both slightly below average. Knowing whether the current level of option volatility is relatively high or low is a key element in long-term option trading success.

Why Mistake #1 Causes Losses in the Long Run

There are two primary problems with relying solely on market timing to trade options:

A) First, picking tops and bottoms for a given underlying security is extremely difficult at best. In fact, many would argue that it is impossible to do on a regular basis.

B) Second, the movement of the price of a given option is not always directly correlated to the price movement of the underlying security. As a result, even if you pick the exact low point for a given stock or futures market and buy a call option, it is still quite possible that the call option you buy will not generate a big profit, or in fact, could actually lose money.

These facts of option trading life are summarily dismissed by the market timer and are major problems among this group of option traders.

The Market Timing Flaw

No matter how "accurate" a trader believes his market timing method to be, the probability of a given underlying security moving in the predicted direction between the time an option is purchased and the expiration date for that option is exactly 50/50. This fact of probability is true even if you are using a trading system that has previously been 80% accurate in predicting the future direction of the underlying security. Despite the fact that 80% of the previous buy signals have been followed by a price advance, the initial probability of the underlying security rising after the next buy signal remains exactly 50/50. Thus, the ardent market timer enters each trade with the flawed perception that the odds are 80/20 in his favor, while in fact they are no better than 50/50. This probability figure regarding price movement applies to the underlying security itself, not to the options on that underlying security, which may fluctuate independently based on several factors that are never considered by the market timer.

Underlying Security Versus Fluctuations in Option Prices

The implied volatility of an option is a key variable in how an option is priced. As explained in Appendix A, each option can trade at its own implied volatility level, and the general level of implied volatilities for the options of a given underlying security can fluctuate widely over time. As a result of these fluctuations in implied volatility, at any given point in time, option premiums may be extremely high, extremely low or anywhere in between. It is essential to long term success to be able to determine whether the current level of implied volatility is high or low for a given underlying security. Lack of this knowledge is the key reason that market timers lose money trading options. At times they pay far too much for the options they buy because they commit one of the cardinal sins of option trading: they assume that the price movement of whatever option they buy will mirror the price movement of the underlying security. Adopting the attitude that "any old option will do" is a sure way to lose money in options.

Ideally you will focus your option buying on situations where implied volatility is relatively low and focus your option writing on situations where implied volatility is relatively high. By doing so you can profit not only from a favorable price movement by the underlying security but also from a favorable change in volatility. One cannot overstate the importance of avoiding option purchases when implied volatility is extremely high.

Any time you buy an option, a subsequent decline in volatility can cause losses in your option position even if the underlying security moves in the predicted direction. This is true whether volatility is high or low at the time you buy an option. However, the higher the implied volatility at the time an option is purchased, the greater the downside risk. If you are walking down the street and trip and fall that is one thing, but if you are standing on a mountain top and you trip and fall that is something entirely different. Clearly if you are standing at the top of a mountain you would likely pay close attention to your footing. The market timer who pays no attention to volatility levels runs the risk of not only falling off of a mountain top, but of not even knowing he is standing on the mountain top at the time he falls. Ignorance clearly is not bliss.

Less Favorable Risk/Reward Relationship

One factor that is often overlooked when buying options is the expected relationship between risk and reward. Because the probability of making money on a long option position if held until expiration is always less than 50% (because of the inevitable time decay of option premiums as they approach expiration), it is very important to a trader's long-term success that he make a lot of money when he is right. In other words, if your probability of making money on each trade is less than 50/50, then if you always have a reward-to-risk ratio of 1 to 1, you will lose money in the long run. As a result, it is extremely important to hit a big winner from time to time. This emphasizes the importance of putting the odds as much on your side as possible in each trade. Unfortunately, the trader who completely ignores implied volatility cannot possibly know if he is maximizing his reward-to-risk potential.

Most traders simply expect to make a lot of money any time they buy an option, so they tend to have an overoptimistic idea about their potential reward. Likewise, by buying an option with limited risk they figure they have little risk — i.e., in their minds the upside potential is so great and the likelihood of losing the entire premium is extremely low. As a result, the perceived reward-to-risk ratio is generally much higher than it actually is in the market place. Let's look at a real world example.

Most traders are trained to trade the underlying security rather than the option. When starting out most traders learn something about technical analysis and/or fundamental analysis. All of this analysis is geared toward determining when to buy or sell a given stock or futures contract. When the decision is made to trade an option on a given underlying security rather than the underlying security itself, many traders mistakenly assume that as long as their timing is good, they can simply buy a call or put and that option will trade exactly as the underlying does. This type of thinking is actually the heart of the problem.

In reality, an option trader's work has only just begun once the timing decision has been made. At that point the trader must decide which option to buy and how to manage the position once it is established. If a trader has two or more underlying securities to choose from, the decision becomes even more complicated. Most traders do not have unlimited capital, so very often they find themselves in a situation where they may have to choose between trading one underlying security for another. Making the proper selections among different underlying securities and determining which option to trade is the step that separates profitable option traders from the other 90%.

Real World Example

A) On April 4 a trader's market timing method gives buy signals on two stocks, US Robotics and Sun Microsystems.

B) Based on these signals, both stocks are expected to rise 10% in the next month.

C) In order to maximize profitability the trader decides to buy a call option on one or the other.

D) The trader has $2500 that he wants to commit to one trade.

The question then is "which stock offers the better option play?" If the trader has no tools other than his market timing method he has no choice but to flip a coin or make a subjective guess. The trader who looks beyond market timing can make a much more enlightened decision that will give him a much greater profit potential.

Figures 3 and 4 display the implied volatility levels for both stocks on the date in question. As you can see, on a relative basis, the implied volatility for US Robotics options is much lower than that of Sun Microsystems. This would suggest that buying "cheap" US Robotics options will offer more potential than buying "expensive" Sun Microsystems options. Let's see if this is true and if so to what extent.

FIGURE 3 - IMPLIED VOLATILITY FOR US ROBOTICS OPTIONS

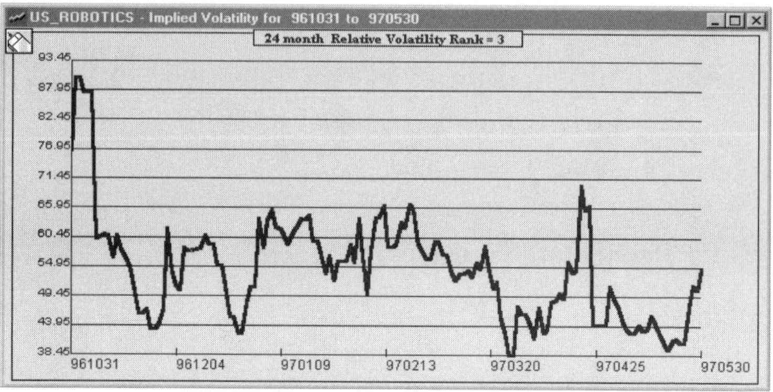

SOURCE: OPTION PRO ON-LINE BY ESSEX TRADING CO., LTD.

FIGURE 4 - IMPLIED VOLATILITY FOR SUN MICROSYSTEMS OPTIONS

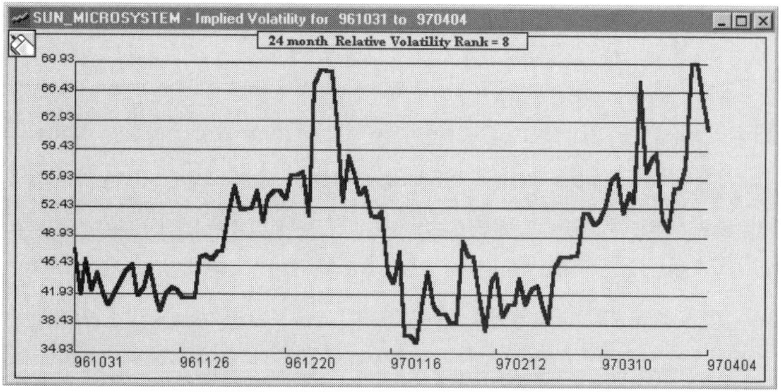

SOURCE: OPTION PRO ON-LINE BY ESSEX TRADING CO., LTD.

Plugging in the following scenario:

A) $2500 of capital.

B) Expecting a 10% advance in price over the next month.

C) Evaluating only "buying calls" strategies.

The expected returns, which appear in Figures 5 and 6, are exactly in line with what we would expect.

FIGURE 5 - EXPECTED RETURNS FOR US ROBOTICS OPTIONS

TradeFinder Output - USRX

	Current Variables	Future Variables
Date	04/04/97	05/05/97
Interest Rate	5	5
Price	58.31	64.12
Volatility	===> Using Actual Implieds	

Trading Capital
2500

Graph Different:
Dates
Volatilities

Double-click on a line to display graph

Market	Suggested Positions	% Profit
US_ROBOTICS	B 9 MAY97 60.C at 2.56	69.6%
US_ROBOTICS	B 4 MAY97 55.C at 5.50	64.3%
US_ROBOTICS	B 2 MAY97 50.C at 9.50	47.2%

SOURCE: OPTION PRO ON-LINE BY ESSEX TRADING CO., LTD.

As you can see in Figures 5 and 6, if the expected scenario plays out — i.e., if US Robotics and Sun Microsystems both rally 10% in the next month — everything else being equal, a trader has a 76% greater potential by taking the US Robotics trade (69% expected profit vs. 39% expected profit).

FIGURE 6 - EXPECTED RETURNS FOR SUN MICROSYSTEMS OPTIONS

TradeFinder Output - SUNW

	Current Variables	Future Variables
Date	04/04/97	05/05/97
Interest Rate	5	5
Price	29.25	32.18
Volatility	===> Using Actual Implieds	

Trading Capital
2500

Graph Different:
Dates
Volatilities

Double-click on a line to display graph

Market	Suggested Positions	% Profit
SUN_MICROSYS	B 13 MAY97 30.C at 1.75	39.0%
SUN_MICROSYS	B 4 MAY97 25.C at 5.12	37.7%
SUN_MICROSYS	B 7 JUL97 30.C at 3.12	35.9%

SOURCE: OPTION PRO ON-LINE BY ESSEX TRADING CO., LTD.

One other factor to consider that makes US Robotics options even more attractive in this situation is the fact that the option volatilities rise and fall fairly regularly. As a result, one additional benefit of buying options when option volatility is low is that there is a greater than average chance that volatility will rise, which will inflate the prices of all options for that security.

For the sake of illustration, let's assume that the implied volatilities for both US Robotics and Sun Microsystems regress to their mean — i.e., both revert to the volatility level that is halfway between their high and low readings. For this to happen, US Robotics, volatility would rise 58.2% from 41.69% to 65.95%.. Conversely, Sun Microsystems, volatility would fall 16% from 62.45% to 52.43%. As you can see in Figures 7 and 8, if the option volatility of both stocks reverted to their mean, the upside potential would be even that much greater for US Robotics options compared to Sun Microsystems. The profit potential for the top US Robotics trade soars to 165% while the profit potential on Sun Microsystems, top trade declines slightly to 37.7%.

FIGURE 7 - EXPECTED RETURNS FOR US ROBOTICS OPTIONS IF IMPLIED VOLATITY REVERTS TO AVERAGE

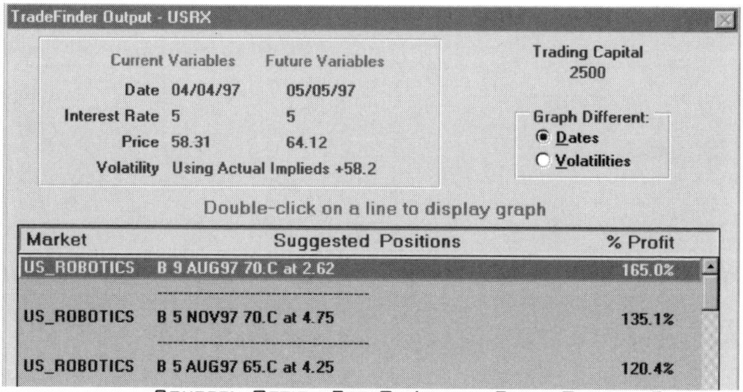

TradeFinder Output - USRX

	Current Variables	Future Variables
Date	04/04/97	05/05/97
Interest Rate	5	5
Price	58.31	64.12
Volatility	Using Actual Implieds +58.2	

Trading Capital
2500

Graph Different:
Dates
Volatilities

Double-click on a line to display graph

Market	Suggested Positions	% Profit
US_ROBOTICS	B 9 AUG97 70.C at 2.62	165.0%
US_ROBOTICS	B 5 NOV97 70.C at 4.75	135.1%
US_ROBOTICS	B 5 AUG97 65.C at 4.25	120.4%

SOURCE: OPTION PRO ON-LINE BY ESSEX TRADING CO., LTD.

FIGURE 8 - EXPECTED RETURNS FOR SUN MICROSYSTEMS OPTIONS IF IMPLIED VOLATILITY REVERTS TO AVERAGE

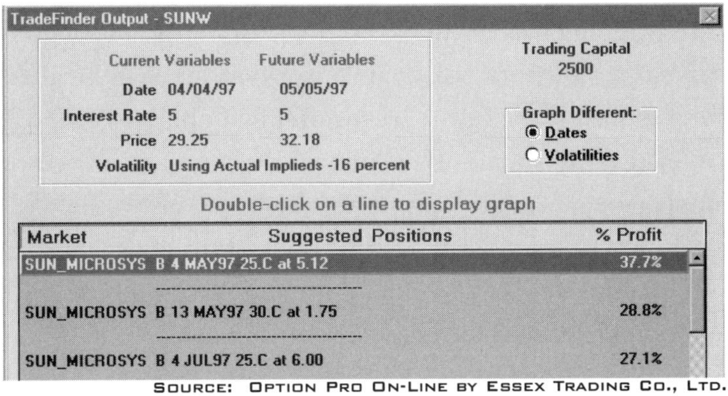

TradeFinder Output - SUNW

	Current Variables	Future Variables
Date	04/04/97	05/05/97
Interest Rate	5	5
Price	29.25	32.18
Volatility	Using Actual Implieds -16 percent	

Trading Capital
2500

Graph Different:
Dates
Volatilities

Double-click on a line to display graph

Market	Suggested Positions	% Profit
SUN_MICROSYS	B 4 MAY97 25.C at 5.12	37.7%
SUN_MICROSYS	B 13 MAY97 30.C at 1.75	28.8%
SUN_MICROSYS	B 4 JUL97 25.C at 6.00	27.1%

SOURCE: OPTION PRO ON-LINE BY ESSEX TRADING CO., LTD.

Not all option trading opportunities are created equal. This example illustrates the importance of not relying solely on market timing to trade options. In this example, the outlook for two different stocks was equally bullish. Yet the trader who bought US Robotics options had much greater upside potential by virtue of buying "cheap" options and the potential for a rise in option volatility. The trader who bought Sun Microsystems calls had much less upside potential. There is also the risk that implied volatility will revert to the average, or worse, fall into low territory, thus deflating all Sun Microsystems option prices.

How To Avoid Mistake #1

Market timing can be an essential part of successful option trading. Unfortunately, the mistake that too many traders make is that they fail to recognize that there is more to option trading success than just market timing. If you do not give serious consideration to which option you buy and how much you pay for it, you set yourself up for losses that could easily have been avoided. Not only can this be bad for your trading account, but making a good market timing call and still losing money can be an extremely damaging experience psychologically.

In order to avoid this mistake you must make a commitment to go the extra step once your market timing mechanism has generated a signal. That extra step involves determining whether implied option volatility is presently high or low for the underlying security and determining which option trading strategy to employ (or not employ) based on this information. One useful technique is to compare the current level of implied volatility with the historical range of volatility for the particular security you are considering, to objectively determine whether the current level is high or low.

The Concept of Relative Volatility

The concept of Relative Volatility ranking allows traders to objectively determine whether the current implied volatility for the options of a given stock or commodity is "high" or "low" on a historical basis. This knowledge is key in determining the best trading strategies to employ for a given security. A simple method for calculating Relative Volatility is simply to note the highest and lowest readings in implied volatility for a given security's options over the last two years (See Appendix A for details on calculating daily implied volatility values for a given security). The difference between the highest and lowest recorded values can then be cut into ten increments, or deciles. If the current implied volatility is in the lowest decile then Relative Volatility is "1." If the current implied volatility is in the highest decile then Relative Volatility is "10." This approach allows traders to make an objective determination as to whether implied option volatility is currently high or low for a given security. They can then use this knowledge to decide which trading strategy to employ as shown in the following tables.

Relative Volatility Rank (1 - 10)

STRATEGY	PROFIT POTENTIAL	RISK	1	2	3	4	5	6	7	8	9	10
Buy Straddles	Unlimited	Limited	X	X								
Buy Naked Options	Unlimited	Limited	X	X	X							
Backspreads	Unlimited	Limited	X	X	X	X	X					
Buy Verticals	Limited	Limited	X	X	X	X	X					
Calendar Spreads	Limited	Limited	X	X	X	X	X					
Sell Verticals	Limited	Limited						X	X	X	X	X
Sell Double Verticals	Limited	Limited							X	X	X	X
Buy Ratio Spreads	Limited	Unlimited								X	X	X
Sell Naked Options	Limited	Unlimited									X	X
Sell Straddles	Limited	Unlimited									X	X

SOURCE: OPTION PRO ON-LINE BY ESSEX TRADING CO., LTD.

Relative Volatility Rank (1 - 10)

HEDGING STRATEGY	PROFIT POTENTIAL	RISK	1	2	3	4	5	6	7	8	9	10
Buy Underlying/ Buy Put	Unlimited	Limited	X	X	X							
Short Underlying/ Buy Call	Limited	Limited	X	X	X							
Buy Underlying/ Sell Call/Buy Put	Limited	Limited				X	X	X	X			
Short Underlying/ Sell Put/Buy Call	Limited	Limited				X	X	X	X			
Buy Underlying/ Sell Call	Limited	Limited								X	X	X
Short Underlying/ Sell Put	Limited	Limited								X	X	X

SOURCE: OPTION PRO ON-LINE BY ESSEX TRADING CO., LTD.

Relative Volatility/Trading Strategy Reference Table

As you can see in the implied volatility graphs displayed in Figures 1, 2 , 3 and 4, implied option volatility can fluctuate widely over time. Traders who are unaware of whether option volatility is currently high or low have no idea if they are paying too much for the options they are buying (or receiving too little for the options that they are writing). This lack of knowledge costs them money in the long run.

Mistake #2
Buying Only Out-Of-The-Money Options

The majority of traders who enter into the options market do so for the express purpose of generating speculative profits. Unlike buying a stock that has some tangible value, a vast number of option traders perceive options more in line with a lottery ticket than as an investment vehicle. In other words, the underlying mentality is the "let's take a shot" mentality. In fact, this is so common that without even doing any research one can realize with a great degree of confidence that this approach is a loser in the long run. Consider this: how many people get rich playing the lottery? How many people make a lot of money in the long run betting on horses? Or blackjack? A few to be sure. But the vast majority of players take their shot, get some excitement, absorb their losses and move on. This is also the case with option traders who focus solely on long shot bets by buying out-of-the-money options (and/or options with little time left until expiration). Let's examine this a little more closely to understand why this is a losing approach.

Why Traders Make Mistake #2

Everybody loves a bargain. Many people love a long shot. And the idea of making a small bet on a long shot for the possibility of a big payoff is exciting to a lot of people. Unfortunately, while this approach to speculation may generate a lot of excitement while the play is being made, in most cases, whether horses, blackjack or options, it invariably leads to losses in the long run. If your primary purpose for speculating truly is to make money, then you must go out of your way to avoid this "lottery syndrome" and should generally avoid long shot bets.

> **Note:**
>
> Before proceeding it should be pointed out that the purpose of this discussion is not to say that you should never "take a shot" in option trading by buying a cheap out-of-the-money option. The purpose is to point out that if this approach makes up the bulk of your trading activity, the odds are overwhelming that you will lose money in the long run.

If you had a choice between betting $200 for the chance of making $1000, or betting $200 for the chance of making $500 which would you choose? Without any more information to go on, the first choice seems an obvious one. A surprising number of option traders take this minimal amount of information and make the "obvious" bet, buying the option with the greater leverage. However, the information that is missing — the probability of achieving the hoped-for return — is the key ingredient in determining long term profitability. To better understand the pitfalls associated with the "long shot" approach to option trading, let's cover some definitions and look at an example.

In-The-Money Option - A call option is "in-the-money" if its strike price is less than the current market price of the underlying. A put option is "in-the-money" if its strike price is higher than the current market price of the underlying.

Out-Of-The-Money Option - An option that currently has no intrinsic value. A call option is "out-of-the-money" if its strike price is higher than the current market price of the underlying. A put option is "out-of-the-money" if its strike price is lower than the current price of the underlying.

Intrinsic Value - The amount by which an option is in-the-money. An out-of-the-money option by definition has no intrinsic value.

Extrinsic Value (or Time Premium) - The price of an option less its intrinsic value. The entire premium of an out-of-the-money option consists of extrinsic value, or "time premium." Time premium is essentially the amount that an option buyer pays to the option seller (above and beyond any intrinsic value of the option) to induce the seller to enter into the trade. All options lose all of their time premium at expiration. This phenomenon is referred to as "time decay."

Hypothetical Example

It is January 31, XYZ stock is trading at $55 a share and there are 3 call options available. The March 50 call is trading at $6, the March 55 call is trading at $3 and the March 60 call is trading at $1. The 50 strike call is "in-the-money" with $5 of intrinsic value and $1 of time premium. The 55 strike call is "at-the-money" and presently has no intrinsic value and is comprised solely of time premium. The 55 strike call will gain one point of intrinsic value for each point that XYZ stock rises above 55. The 60 strike call is "out-of-the-money," has no intrinsic value, is comprised solely of time premium and will not gain any intrinsic value until XYZ stock trades above $60.

January 31 - Stock trading at 55
March Call Options

Strike	Profit Price	Delta	Intrinsic Value	Time Premium	Price at Expiration*
50	6	82	5	1	5
55	3	50	0	3	0
60	1	26	0	1	0

* - IF STOCK PRICE IS STILL 55 AT OPTION EXPIRATION

Assume that you are bullish on this stock and expect an advance in price in the weeks ahead. The obvious question then is "which is the better option to buy?" The response to this question varies, but the thought process is almost universal. Each trader makes a subjective determination in their head as to which option is best without thoroughly examining the risk/reward characteristics of each choice. The "shooters" invariably like the 60 call because it only costs $100. "The most I can lose is $100. What a deal." The opportunity to buy something at a low price is almost too much to pass up for some people. And so it is in option trading. Very often when a trader is looking to buy an option there is an overwhelming temptation to buy a far out-of-the-money option simply because the cost of the option is so cheap. The trader figures, "if I'm right, I'll make a killing and if I'm wrong I'll only lose a little." Unfortunately, because this approach completely ignores probability, nine times out of ten, it is the trader who gets killed in the long run if this is his primary strategy for trading options.

Why Mistake #2 Causes Losses in the Long Run

Not everything that seems to be a bargain actually is one. The danger in buying something simply because of its low price is that all too often "you get what you pay for." The primary problem with buying far out-of-the-money options is that you may be inadvertently stacking the odds against yourself.

Probability is an extremely important factor in option trading success. When buying an option, traders can approximate the probability that the option they are purchasing will expire "in-the-money" by checking the "delta" value for the option they are purchasing. A "delta" value is calculated by an option pricing model for each individual option. The delta value can range from 0 to 100 for calls and from 0 to -100 for puts. The significance of a particular option's delta value can be viewed in three different and instructive ways:

A) First, the delta value for a given option indicates the probability that the option will expire "in-the-money." Thus, an option with a delta of 20 presently has a 20% probability of expiring in-the-money.

B) Second, a delta value of 20 implies that if the underlying stock increases one full point, the option will increase in value by 0.20.

C) Third, a delta value of 100 indicates that the option position is currently the equivalent of holding 100 shares of stock (or being long one futures contract). Thus, buying a put option with a delta of -40 means the position is equivalent to being short 40 shares of the underlying stock (or being short 4/10's of one futures contract).

A delta value of 50 for an at-the-money call option indicates that there is a 50/50 chance that that option will be in-the-money at expiration. Accordingly, in-the-money options have deltas greater than 50 and out-of-the-money options have deltas less than 50.

Referring back to our earlier example using XYZ stock, the 50 call had a delta of 82, the 55 call had a delta of 50 and the 60 call had a delta of 26. This tells us that there is an 82% probability that XYZ stock will be above 50 when the March options expire, a 50% probability of being above 55 and only a 26% probability of being above 60. In other words, there is a 74% chance that the 60 call option will expire as worthless. Make no mistake about it — these are long odds. Unfortunately, this crucial information often is overlooked or easily dismissed by a trader who has adopted the "what the heck, the most I can lose is $100" approach.

To make matters worse for the "shooter," the delta value only measures the probability of the underlying stock reaching the strike price for the option. Because you also pay time premium your target price is actually higher when buying calls (lower when buying puts), which in turn reduces even further your probability of showing a profit if the option is held until expiration. For example, buying the 60 call option in our example for $1 (or $100) means that your effective break-even price for the underlying stock is 61 (the 60 strike price plus the cost of the option). The probability of the stock being at 61 or higher by March option expiration (in this example) is 19%.

To spell it out, if you buy the 60 call for $1, you have less than a 1 in 5 chance of breaking even (before commissions) if you hold this option until expiration. That statement of the facts graphically illustrates what is at the heart of Mistake #2: If the bulk of your option trading involves making bets with less than a 20% probability of profit, the odds are overwhelming that you will lose money in the long run. Let's do some more math to fully drive home this point. If four out of every five trades lose $100, then you must make $400 on the fifth trade simply to stay even. As we refer again to our example, XYZ stock would have to rise to 65 at expiration in order for the 60 call bought at $1 to generate a $400 profit (again, this example excludes commissions that raise the bar even higher in the real world of trading). The probability of this stock reaching 65 at the time of March option expiration is only 8%. Good luck.

Let's discuss one last issue on this topic just to cover all the bases. The common defensive retort of a "shooter" after being presented with these facts is to say "well I don't plan to hold the option until expiration. I'm going to hit a big winner and get out." For arguments sake, let's examine this line of thinking. Let's assume that the trader entering this March call trade on January 31 wants to be out by February 28. Based on computer testing, XYZ stock would have to be above 57⅞ on that date in order for the 60 call to show a profit (again, before commissions). What is the probability of this stock, currently trading at 55, rising to 57⅞ four weeks later? In this case the probability is 28%. So basically, the hope of simply breaking even still amounts to a long shot bet. The best case scenario for the "shooter" is an immediate movement in the anticipated direction by the underlying security. In order for the 60 call in our example to generate the $400 profit this trader needs to make in order to cover the $100 he loses on his four out of five losers, XYZ would need to advance to 58 by February 7. The probability of this happening is just 12%.

Real World Example

At times buying options just one strike price apart can make the difference between profit and loss. On April 4 Merck stock was trading at 86⅞.

April 4 - Merck stock trading at 86⅞
May Call Options

Strike	Profit Price	Delta	Intrinsic Value	Time Premium	Price at Expiration*
85	4.50	63	1.88	2.62	1.88
90	2.25	39	0.00	2.25	0.00

* - IF STOCK PRICE IS STILL 86⅞ AT OPTION EXPIRATION

A trader who is bullish on Merck stock may consider one of three possible trades:

A) Buy 100 shares of Merck stock (cost = $8688).

B) Buy 19 May 85 call options (cost = $8550).

C) Buy 38 May 90 call options (cost = $8550).

The "shooter" is immediately drawn to the prospect of buying the 90 calls. By doing so he can buy twice as many options as if he bought the 85 call. This gives him the greatest profit potential if Merck stock rallies sharply. However, with options there is always a trade-off. The trade-off between buying an in-the-money option and an out-of-the-money option is this:

A) The out-of-the-money option always offers greater leverage if the underlying security makes a major price move.

B) The in-the-money option always offers a higher probability of making money than the out-of-the-money option.

The factors that the "shooter" who immediately jumps at the out-of-the-money option fails to consider are:

A) The probability of his best case scenario working out.

B) How the worst case scenario will affect his position.

Look at Figures 9 and 10. These charts display the P\L curves for the 85 call option and the 90 call option at expiration. (The price of the stock is plotted along the bottom of the graph and the dollar profit or loss is plotted down the side of the graph.) There are several important factors to note when comparing these two positions. The 90 call clearly has the greatest upside potential if Merck stock rallies sharply. Unfortunately, if that is the only factor a trader takes into consideration he misses several other key factors.

In the "Cursor Position" window in Figure 9, you will note that the break-even price for this trade is 89.50. The probability of Merck stock being above this price at the time of option expiration is 38%. In the "Cursor Position" window in Figure 10, you will note that the break-even price for this trade is 92.25. The probability of Merck stock being above this price at the time of option expiration is 28%.

FIGURE 9 - EXPECTED P\L CURVE FOR MERCK MAY 85 CALL OPTION AT EXPIRATION

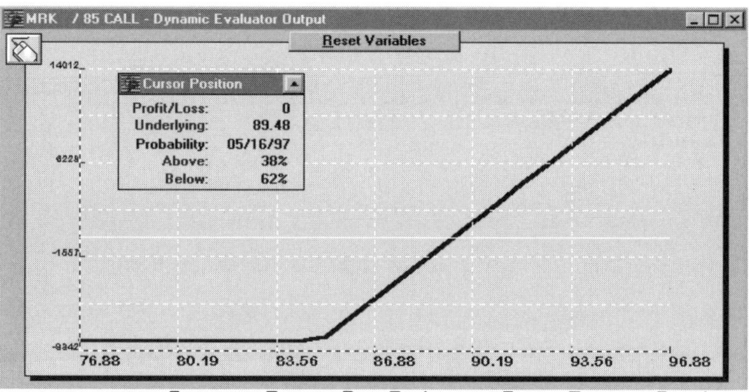

SOURCE: OPTION PRO ON-LINE BY ESSEX TRADING CO., LTD.

The trader in this example must decide which is more important to him — greater upside potential or a higher probability of profit. There is no exact right or wrong answer to this question. However, the problem is that too many traders never ask this question! They simply go for the greatest leverage without regard to the other important factors.

FIGURE 10 - EXPECTED P\L CURVE FOR MERCK MAY 90 CALL OPTION AT EXPIRATION

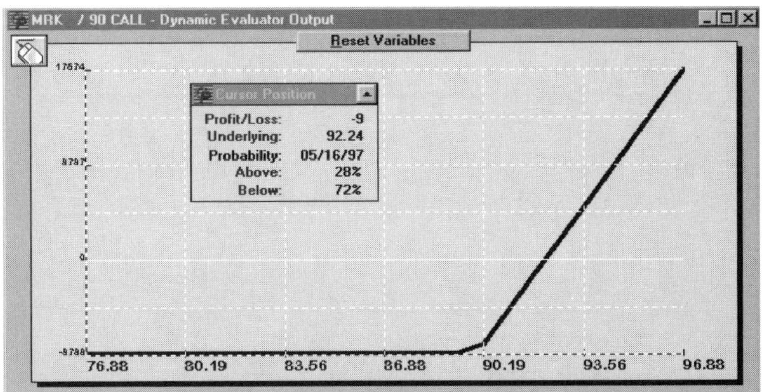

SOURCE: OPTION PRO ON-LINE BY ESSEX TRADING CO., LTD.

Between April 4 and May 16 (the expiration date for the May options), Merck stock rallied 5% from 86⅞ to 91¼. The trader who simply bought 100 shares of Merck stock made \$437 on an \$8688 investment, or 5%. As shown in Figure 11, the trader who bought the 85 call made \$3150 on an \$8550 investment, or 37%. This illustrates the possibility of leveraging your gains using options. However, the danger with using leverage is that you may employ too much leverage. As shown in Figure 12, the trader who bought the 90 call because it offered the greatest leverage actually lost \$4512 on his \$8550 investment, for a loss of 53%!

FIGURE 11 - ACTUAL RESULTS FOR MERCK MAY 85 CALL OPTION (+$3150)

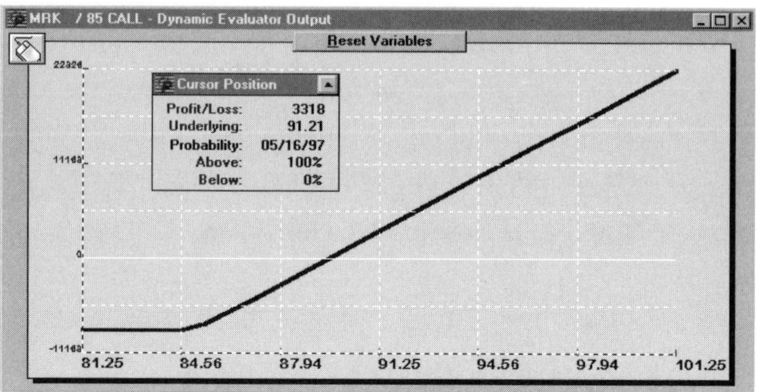

SOURCE: OPTION PRO ON-LINE BY ESSEX TRADING CO., LTD.

Stock rises 5%, option trader makes 37%

FIGURE 12 - ACTUAL RESULTS FOR MERCK MAY 90 CALL OPTION (-$4512)

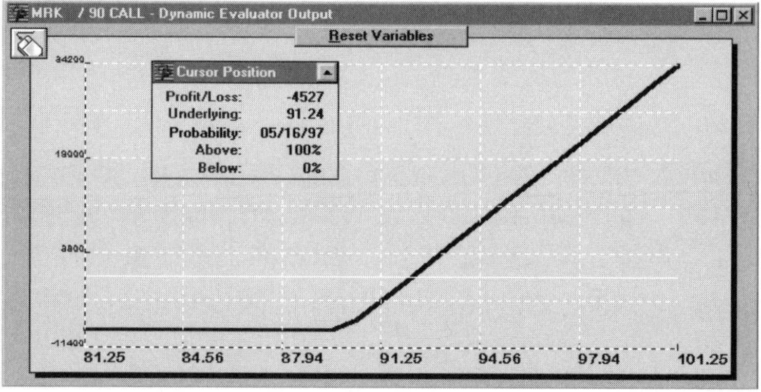

SOURCE: OPTION PRO ON-LINE BY ESSEX TRADING CO., LTD.

Stock rises 5%, option trader loses 53%

How To Avoid Mistake #2

The trap that many option traders fall into is that they feel that their best move in trading options is to obtain the maximum amount of leverage possible. In other words, "I'm trading a speculative vehicle for the purpose of leveraging my gains. I might as well go for the gusto." This approach invariably leads to losses in the long run. The good news is that the answer to this problem is really very simple. The bad news is that the answer essentially "rains on the parade" of a lot of traders who start out trading options with the notion of earning "incredible" profits.

The way to make money buying options in the long run is to avoid trying to make all the money in the world in the short run. In short, the key is to reduce the amount of leverage you use when buying options.

The killer in options trading is time decay. If you buy an at-the-money option and hold it until expiration you generally have only about a 1 in 3 chance of breaking even before slippage and commissions. Most traders would be better off reducing their leverage and buying options that have some intrinsic value, rather than just buying cheap out-of-the-money options that will more than likely expire as completely worthless. In an interview in Technical Analysis of Stocks and Commodities magazine, Larry McMillan, the author of "Options as a Strategic Investment" and "McMillan On Options" talked about buying options with a delta of 70 or more. In other words, rather than buying a cheap option comprised solely of time premium which will likely expire as worthless, his suggestion was to treat options as more like a substitute for the underlying security.

A trader looking at XYZ stock in our example could put up $5,500 to buy 100 shares of stock. As an alternative, he could buy a call option. The trader could spend just $100 and buy the 60 call option, thus obtaining leverage of 55 to 1. This sounds great until you remember that he will have about a 1 in 5 chance of making money on the trade. Another choice would be to reduce the amount of leverage while greatly increasing the probability of making money. By buying the 50 call option for $600, he still obtains substantial leverage over simply buying the stock, in this case about 9 to 1. Also, once the stock rises above 56, he would profit point-for-point with the stock itself. Unfortunately, too many investors pass up leverage of 9 to 1 with good odds to "shoot for the moon" with the option offering leverage of 55 to 1, despite the overwhelmingly unfavorable odds.

Because of the negative effects of probability and time decay when buying options, in the long run you stand a much greater chance of trading profitably by reducing your leverage and buying options with some intrinsic value rather than always "taking shots" with out-of-the money options.

Mistake #3
Using Strategies That Are Too Complex

The majority of option traders who fail fall into the "market timing" and/or "buy cheap options for maximum leverage" traps. However, there are other approaches to option trading that seem to lure in a particular type of trader. While many traders are turned on by buying cheap options in the hopes of making untold sums, other traders enter the options market from the opposite end of the spectrum, that being the "low risk" approach. Option trading offers numerous opportunities to traders, speculators, investors and hedgers. You can enter into a position that profits if a stock rises above a given price, stays below a given price, stays above one price and below another price, moves above one price or below another price, and any other number of possibilities.

With all of this flexibility comes a certain level of complexity. A "complex" strategy can be defined as any trade that involves more than one option. Defining the point at which a strategy becomes "too complex" can only be done on an individual basis. A strategy that is "too complex" basically is one that a trader enters into without fully understanding either why or how he is going to profit, and/or without a full understanding of the risks involved.

Why Traders Make Mistake #3

The most common reason people trade complex strategies is because they have somehow been led to believe that they "can't lose," or that a given strategy entails "low risk" or a "high probability of profit." Normally it results from hearing about some strategy that captures their imagination. The most well known example of this type of trading is referred to as "delta neutral" trading. Very often traders attempt to position trades so that they are "delta neutral." This simply means putting on a combination of option (and possibly underlying) positions so that when the positive and negative deltas are added together, the net result is as close to zero as possible. As long as a position is "delta neutral" it essentially has no bias in regards to the price movement of the underlying security.

IMPORTANT NOTE

The purpose of the following discussion is not to denigrate delta neutral trading. The concept is sound and can be profitable in the long run if implemented and monitored properly. The purpose of the discussion is simply to present a few common examples of trades that novice traders often enter into without fully understanding the potential implications of what they are doing.

A delta neutral position can be entered into in a variety of ways. The most common approach is to sell a far out-of-the-money call and a far out-of-the-money put with roughly equivalent deltas (call delta values are positive and put delta values are negative; thus selling a call with a delta of 10 and a put with a delta of -10 results in a delta neutral position). Another approach is to buy 100 shares of stock (which have a delta of 100) and buy two put options with a delta of -50, once again resulting in a delta neutral position. Despite the fact that both of these examples represent delta neutral trades, they are very different positions. The first trade will be profitable if the underlying security remains in a range; the second will profit only if the underlying security moves far enough in one direction or the other.

Why Mistake #3 Causes Losses in the Long Run

There is nothing inherently wrong with trading "complex" option strategies. The problem comes when traders start entering multi-layered trades without fully understanding the risk/reward dynamics involved.

To illustrate this, let's consider an example. Many option professionals like to tout the virtues of selling delta neutral strangles, a strategy that involves selling out-of-the-money call and put options and then hoping that the underlying security stays in a range so that the options expire as worthless. "90% probability of profit" is a common banner for this type of trading idea. And in fact the claim may be entirely true. Selling a call with a delta of 10 and a put with a delta of -10 can place you into a position that indeed has a 90% probability of profit. In other words, based on probability there is a 90% chance that at the time the options expire, the underlying security will be above the put option strike price and below the call option strike price, thus resulting in a profitable trade.

Many conservative traders are drawn to this type of approach because of the favorable odds. However, if you fail to properly examine the risk/reward dynamics of this trade you may not realize that you are entering into a trade that has a limited profit potential (limited to the amount of premium you collect when you write the options) and unlimited risk (if the market moves too far in either direction). Additionally, this strategy may require a great deal of margin for your broker to allow you to hold the trade. There are several things to consider before entering into complex trading strategies.

There Is No Such Thing As A "Risk-Free" Trade

Regardless of what anybody tells you, there is no such thing as "risk-free" trading. With options, everything is a trade-off. If you buy a cheap out-of-the-money option you may have a small dollar risk but you may also have only a 10% probability of actually making money. On the other end of the spectrum, if you sell a naked out-of-the-money call option you may have a 90% probability of making money, but you also are exposed to unlimited risk if for some unforeseen reason the underlying security makes an explosive move in the wrong direction.

Entering into a trade with a 90% probability of making money is very comforting to many traders. However, once this trade is actually entered, the relevant question is no longer "what is my probability of making money?" The relevant question becomes "what am I going to do if the market moves sharply against me and I am faced with a loss?" If the underlying market rallies sharply the trader in this example MUST act to cut his loss, regardless of his initial "probability of profit."

> Rule of Thumb for option trading strategies and life in general:
>
> *If it sounds too good to be true, it is.*

If You Sell Premium, Slippage and Commissions Eat Away At Profits

A number of option strategies attempt to take advantage of time decay by selling options. This can be a very profitable approach. One of the negatives to consider, however, is the effect of slippage and commissions. Slippage is simply the difference between the price you expect to be filled at and the price at which you actually are filled. If you are using market orders to trade thinly traded options, slippage can be substantial. If you are taking in an amount of premium that represents your maximum profit on the trade, it is important to keep slippage and commissions to a minimum so that they do not eat up too large of a portion of your profits.

Do You Have A Clear Objective for Entering the Trade?

A given trade might require the underlying security to rally to a certain level or remain in a certain range in order to generate a profit. Do you have a reason to believe that this will occur? Also, any time you enter into an option trade you should know what your break-even price (or prices in some cases) is for the underlying security. In other words, "this position will be profitable if XYZ stays between 50 and 60." You may also need to know at what point your profit is capped and certainly what your maximum dollar risk is as well as the price the underlying security would have to reach in order to generate unacceptable losses.

Recognize That Adjustments To Position May Be Required

Ideally you will enter into a trade and then simply wait for your profits to start rolling in. However, it doesn't always work that way. Often option positions must be adjusted if certain risk points are reached. This is particularly true for delta neutral trades. Option deltas change as the underlying market price moves. Thus a trade that is delta neutral today may not be delta neutral tomorrow and may require a trader to adjust, or "re-balance" the position by closing out some positions and/or opening others to once again achieve delta neutrality.

This is not an issue to take lightly. With certain types of trading you must be prepared to make adjustments exactly when they are needed. This involves planning in advance for each contingency and even more importantly, having the discipline to pull the trigger in the heat of battle. Another factor to consider is that each time you adjust a position you are subject to more commissions and potentially additional slippage. As stated earlier, if the strategy you are using entails limited profit potential, trading costs can significantly reduce your profit potential.

Adjustments May Be Subjective

Here is another potential problem, especially for inexperienced traders. Say a trader sells an out-of-the-money call and an out-of-the-money put and decides to adjust the position if the underlying security moves within one strike price of either option. Assume further that the underlying security subsequently rallies to within one strike price of the call the trader sold originally. What should the trader do now? Adjust the position? Sure that was the plan. But what is the "right" adjustment to make? He can close out the entire position, he can close out the calls (possibly at a loss), he can close out the calls and sell further out-of-the-money calls, he can do that and also close out the puts and sell puts with a higher strike price than those originally sold, or some other variation. There is no one answer that is always "correct."

What it boils down to is this: At the worst possible moment (i.e., when the trade is reaching the danger level) the trader will need to reassess the relative merits of a number of options and make a decision in fairly short order as to how best to adjust his position. This is by no means impossible. It does however, leave a huge amount of room for error for even a veteran professional option trader, let alone a novice who thought he was getting into a trade that was 90% certain to make money.

Failure To Adjust May Lead to One Huge Loss That Wipes Out A Lot of Small Gains

It is not uncommon to hear of traders who had 90% winning trades (usually selling far out-of-the-money options for small profits) only to get wiped out by one bad trade because they failed to cut their loss when the market moved against them. The only way to avoid this fate is to have a plan and stick to it.

It Can Be Very Difficult To Keep Break-Even/Adjustment Points Straight

One recently touted strategy involves selling short 10 S&P 500 futures contracts and buying 20 at-the-money call options to achieve a delta neutral position. Subsequently, any time that the net delta reaches 100 or -100 the position is adjusted so that it is once again delta neutral. Like anything else, under the right circumstance this strategy can work wonderfully. The relevant question however is "can you make the commitment to follow this position on an ongoing basis in order to make the proper adjustments whenever they are required?" A trader needs to give himself a very honest answer to this question before entering into this type of trading.

Example

Example of a Delta Neutral Position

On May 1 June 97 S&P futures were trading at 802.05
Sell 2 May 835 Calls @ 110 = (Delta 9 (Total Delta of -18
Sell 2 May 755 Puts @ 185 = (Delta -9 (Total Delta of +18
Total Position Delta is -0-

If held until the May options expire on May 15, this delta neutral trade will show a profit if the June S&P is trading anywhere between 752.20 and 838.00 as shown in Figure 13.

At the time this trade is considered there is a 90% probability that the S&P will remain within this profit zone. This is exactly the type of "high probability, low risk" trade that entices many traders. The problem, however, is when a trader enters this trade banking on a high probability of profit without also analyzing the risk side of the equation.

FIGURE 13 - P\L CURVE FOR S&P 500 DELTA NEUTRAL TRADE (WHEN THE TRADE WAS ENTERED)

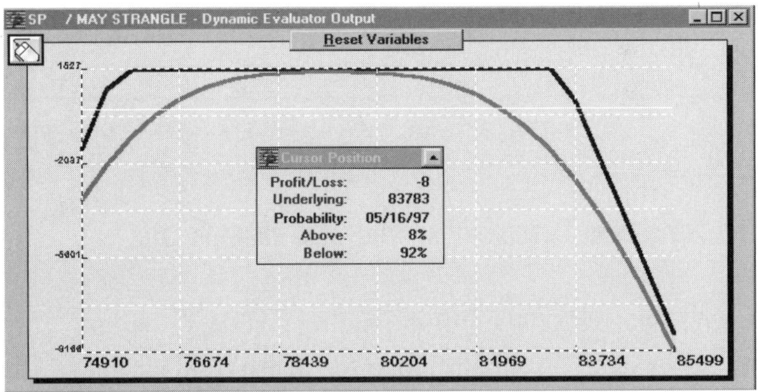

SOURCE: OPTION PRO ON-LINE BY ESSEX TRADING CO., LTD.

Move Forward One Week

On May 8 (one week later) June 97
S&P futures are trading at 822.55
2 May 835 Calls are now 480 = (Delta 31 (Total Delta of -62
2 May 755 Puts are now 35 = (Delta -1 (Total Delta of +2
Total Position Delta is -60

You now have a loss ($1100 before transaction costs), AND you're no longer delta-neutral!

If the futures keep rising, large unlimited losses can occur!

FIGURE 14 - P\L CURVES FOR S&P 500 DELTA NEUTRAL TRADE (ONE WEEK LATER)

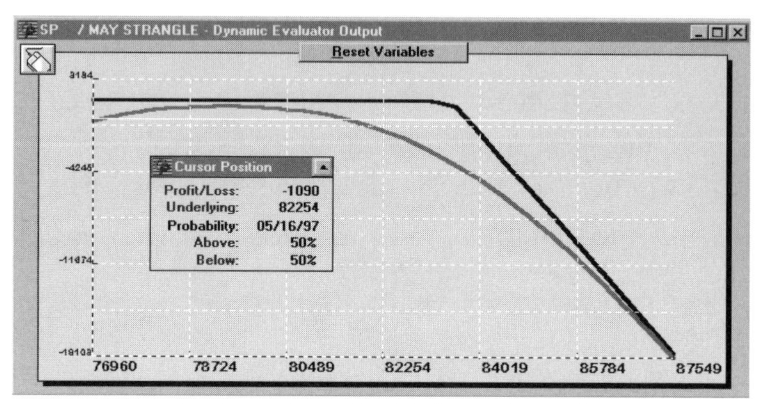

SOURCE: OPTION PRO ON-LINE BY ESSEX TRADING CO., LTD.

The key points to remember from this example are:

A) There are NO option trading strategies, simple or complex, that guarantee profits, no matter how favorable the odds, AND;

B) Every trading strategy has advantages and disadvantages. If you enter any trade for which you are not aware of the potential negative factors involved and/or are unprepared to deal with these negatives factors, you are trading with a strategy that is too complex.

How To Avoid Mistake #3

As discussed earlier, only the individual trader can accurately assess when his or her trading is becoming too complex. The main considerations regarding a particular trade are:

- What is my objective for entering into this trade?
- What is my maximum profit potential and the probability of achieving it?
- What is my maximum risk and the probability of experiencing that?
- Will I need to adjust this position?
- If so, at what point will I need to adjust and what type of adjustment will be required?
- Am I going to be able to keep close enough track of this trade to avoid any potential disasters?

If you cannot answer these questions regarding a particular trade before you enter the trade, that should tell you not to take the trade in the first place.

Mistake #4
Casting Too Wide of a Net

One thought that crosses the minds of a lot of option traders goes something like this, "I want to scan every option of every stock and/or futures contract to find the best one to trade." In other words, they believe that looking at every option is the best way to find the best option trades.

Why Traders Make Mistake #4

It sounds like a logical idea. "Certainly if I analyzed every option then I would find the best trades." Unfortunately, there are a number of holes in this theory. First, from a psychological point-of-view, most traders share an unspoken belief that the best trade is "out there somewhere, if only I could find it." Since it is so cumbersome a task to scan every option of every stock and/or futures market, it is almost a built-in excuse to say "if only I could do that then I would be a winning trader."

Why Mistake #4 Causes Losses in the Long Run

In most endeavors if you try to do too much you invariably wind up biting off more than you can chew. This is also applicable to option trading. The good news is that in option trading you actually are better off if you narrow the focus rather than try to expand it.

You Cannot Look At A Particular Option and Say It Is A Good One To Trade

It is not possible to look at the price of a given option in a vacuum and say, "yes, this is a good option to trade." Every option will react in a slightly different way to a given move in the underlying security. In order to make a realistic assessment of the benefits of buying or writing a given option, you must have some future scenario in mind to properly determine the prospects for a particular trade. This generally involves either some type of market timing forecast or some outlook for a change in volatility levels, either up or down.

Limitations of Analysis of Actual vs. Theoretical

Another common refrain among novice traders is "I want to look at all the options so I can find the most undervalued options to buy (or overvalued options to sell)." What this refers to is the difference between the theoretical price of a given option, which is calculated by an option pricing model, and the actual market price of the option. If the actual price is below the theoretical price then the option is considered to be "undervalued." Likewise, if the actual price is above the theoretical price then the option is considered to be "overvalued." Traders often believe that they can gain an edge by buying "undervalued" options and/or selling "overvalued" options. This is true to a limited extent, but there are a number of caveats involved:

- Just because an option is trading below its theoretical value, there is no assurance that it will go up in price. If a particular call is undervalued and the underlying security declines in price and/or volatility declines, the price of the option will decline no matter how undervalued it may appear.

- Just because an option is trading above its theoretical value there is no assurance that it will go down in price. If a particular call is overvalued and the underlying security advances in price and/or volatility increases, the price of the option will increase no matter how overvalued it may appear.

- Implied option volatility levels can fluctuate widely over time. Everything else being equal, you are generally better off buying an overvalued option when implied volatility levels are low than you are buying undervalued options when implied volatility levels are extremely high.

- Taking advantage of option mispricings is generally best left to floor traders who have instant access and minimal trading costs, and to huge arbitrageurs who do nothing but look for such opportunities. The small trader is almost certain to lose in the long run if he gets into the game of trying to take 1/8, and 1/4's out of the option market.

- There are different option pricing models available, Black/Scholes, Binomial, Cox/Rubenstein, etc., and different models may generate different theoretical prices for the same option. One model may indicate that a given option is overvalued whereas a different model may tell you that the same option is considered fairly valued.

- The biggest limitation in considering theoretical option prices is that they don't really matter much when you get away from theory and into the real world of trading. For example, say that three different option models generate three different theoretical prices for the same option — 5.63, 5.74 and 5.86, respectively. When you go to buy this option in the real world you may find that the Bid price is 5.50 and the Ask price is 6.00. The market makers on the floor don't care where you think the option should be priced. If you want to trade this option right now, you can either buy it at 6.00 or sell it at 5.50. Those are your choices in the real world.

Here is the bottom line regarding Actual versus Theoretical prices. In general you should try to avoid buying an option that is trading far above its theoretical value and you should also avoid selling an option that is selling far below its theoretical value. Beyond that you should pay far more attention to likely underlying price movements, implied volatility levels, trading volume and bid and ask prices than to theoretical option prices.

Lack Of Trading Volume Makes Most Options Difficult To Trade

If you look closely at a newspaper that reports option prices as well as option volume, you will notice something interesting. Most options trade very little volume on a daily basis. In fact, many don't trade at all. Still, there is a price quoted for the option. Many traders assume that if the option price is in the paper, it's just as good as any other option in the paper and that they can buy or sell as many as they want at that price.

Unfortunately, the difference between theory and reality is huge when it comes to trading. Seeing a price quoted for a particular option and believing that it offers a good trading opportunity can be a far cry from actually going into the marketplace and getting filled at that quoted price. Option market makers often joke about options that trade "by invitation only." What this implies is that you need to "look behind the curtain" and see if there is any trading actually going on in an option that you are looking to trade. When looking at options for a stock or futures market you've never traded before, call your broker and ask for the bid/ask spread on a few options. If the bid/ask spread is wide, you may want to avoid trading in that market.

How To Avoid Mistake #4

One thing that should be evident by now in option trading is that if something seems easy or logical, it should probably be questioned. Most traders do what seems easiest or most logical. It's interesting then that 90% of option traders lose money in the long run. It seems logical to want to cast a bigger net and try to follow more stocks or futures markets. But in reality, most traders would be much better off by narrowing the focus, rather than trying to widen it. To make money in options you need trading opportunities. In order to take advantage of a trading opportunity you need someone to take the other side of your trade at a reasonable price. This requires trading volume. As a result, traders should focus their efforts on those stocks and futures markets that offer the greatest option trading liquidity. Figure 15 presents a list of 19 stocks and 12 futures markets that tend to have consistently high option trading volume.

By focusing on these markets you will probably find more trading opportunities than you can use (and more time to devote to each security than if you tried to cover every available stock or futures market), and more importantly, you will be able to actually take advantage of these trades in the marketplace. Most traders find a stock or futures market that they want to trade and then look at the options. However, if you plan to trade options actively, you will benefit in three ways if you start by focusing on only those securities that consistently have high option trading volume.

The Benefits of Narrowing The Focus:

A) You will spend less time trying to sift through every option of every imaginable security looking for that "one great trade" and will have more time to devote to meaningful analysis of a handful of securities.

B) Once you narrow the focus chances are you will be amazed at how you find yourself discovering more trading opportunities than you can actually use.

C) When the time comes to actually make an option trade, you will find market makers offering a spread of 1/8 of a point rather than 1/2 point or more for illiquid options. This difference alone will save you a great deal of money in the long run.

FIGURE 15 - STOCKS & FUTURES MARKETS WITH ACTIVE OPTION VOLUME

STOCKS WITH ACTIVE OPTION TRADING	FUTURES WITH ACTIVE OPTION TRADING
APPLE COMPUTER	CORN
CISCO SYSTEM	CRUDE OIL
COCA COLA	D-MARK
COMPAQ	GOLD
DELL COMPUTER	HEATING OIL
HEWLETT-PACKARD	JAPANESE YEN
IBM	NATURAL GAS
INTEL	S&P 500
IOMEGA	SOYBEANS
MICRON TECHNOLOGY	T-BONDS
MICROSOFT	10-YEAR T-NOTES
MOTOROLA	5-YEAR T-NOTES
OEX	
ORACLE	
PHILIP MORRIS	
SPX	
SUN MICROSYSTEMS	
TEXAS INSTRUMENTS	
THREE COM	

Summary

The traits most often associated with option trading are limited risk, unlimited potential, leverage and the ability to tailor a position to fit a particular objective. The good news is that all of these traits accurately portray the opportunities available when trading options. The bad news is that options by their very nature are a complex subject, which leaves a great deal of room for error. In order to succeed a trader must do the homework required to fully understand what his or her true objectives are and to devise and follow a plan that has a realistic expectation of achieving those objectives. Unfortunately, because of the complex nature of options many traders find it easier to simply follow the most common approaches to trading, without really considering the likelihood of a profitable outcome in the long run. "If everybody else is doing it, it must be right" is a common thought. However, when you are talking about an endeavor where 90% of the participants wind up losing in the long run, the opposite is actually true.

The most difficult step in becoming a profitable options trader is realizing and accepting that the "usual" approaches to option trading followed by the majority of traders lead to losses, and that a trader must ardently avoid the common pitfalls if he hopes to profit in the long run. The table below presents a brief summary of the mistakes we have detailed, why they lead to losses and what a trader needs to do in order to avoid these problems.

Summary Table

MISTAKE	WHY THIS CAUSES FAILURE	HOW TO AVOID IT
1 Relying Solely On Market Timing	Ignores implied volatility; can lead to paying far too much to purchase options	Carefully analyze which option (or options) are best suited to achieve your objective
2 Buying Only Out-Of-the-Money Options	Ignores probability; leads to buying options with little likelihood of profiting	Consider the likelihood of making money on a given trade before getting in
3 Using Strategies That Are Too Complex	Leads to unfavorable risk\reward situations	Determine your objective and make certain the trade you are going to make can achieve those objectives without more risk than you can handle
4 Casting Too Wide a Net	Too much time wasted looking for opportunities among illiquid options	Focus on securities that have actively traded options

Option trading can generate substantial profits if you avoid the common mistakes and adopt an intelligent approach to trading. Avoiding the mistakes detailed in this guide is a good first step.

Appendix A.

Calculating Implied Volatility For a Given Option

There are several variables that enter into an option pricing model to arrive at a theoretical price, or "fair value," of a given option:

A) The current price of the underlying security

B) The strike price of the option under analysis

C) Current interest rates

D) The number of days until the option expires

E) A volatility value

Elements A through E are passed to an option pricing model, which then generates:

F) A theoretical option price

Elements A, B, C and D are "known" variables. In other words, at a given point in time one can readily observe the underlying price, the strike price for the option in question, the current level of interest rates and the number of days until the option expires. To calculate the implied volatility of a given option we follow the procedure above with one modification. Instead of passing elements A through E to an option pricing model to have the model generate a "theoretical" price, we pass elements A through D along with the actual market price for the option as variable F, and allow the option pricing model to solve for element E, the volatility value. A computer is needed to make this calculation. This volatility value is called the "implied volatility" for that option. In other words, it is the volatility that is implied by the marketplace based on the actual price of the option. For example, on 12/1/95 the IBM January 1996 95 Call option was trading at a price of 4.00. The known variables are:

A) The current price of the underlying security = 94.75
B) The strike price of the option under analysis = 95
C) Current interest rates = 5
D) The number of days until the option expires = 50
E) Volatility = ?
F) The actual market price of the option = 4.00

The unknown variable that must be solved for is element E, volatility. Given the variables listed above, a volatility of 27.13 must be plugged into element E in order for the option pricing model to generate a theoretical price that equals the actual market price of 4.00 (this value of 27.13 can only be calculated by passing the other variables into an option pricing model). Thus, the "implied volatility" for the IBM January 1996 95 Call is 27.13 as of the close on 12/1/95. Different options may trade at different implied volatility levels. If demand in the marketplace is great for a given option, the price of that option may be driven to artificially high levels, thus generating a higher implied volatility for that option. The differences in implied volatilities across strike prices among options of the same expiration month for a given underlying are referred to as the volatility "skew."

Implied Volatility For a Given Security

While each option for a given market may trade at its own implied volatility level, it is possible to objectively arrive at a single value to refer to as the average implied volatility value for the options of a given security for a specific day. This daily value can then be compared to the historical range of implied volatility values for that security to determine if this current reading is "high" or "low." The preferred method is to calculate the average implied volatility of the at-the-money call and put for the nearest expiration month, which has at least two weeks until expiration, and refer to that as the implied volatility for that market. The at-the-money options are generally the most actively traded and serve as a reliable reference point when approximating option volatility levels for a given market. For example, if on December 1, IBM is trading at 95 and the implied volatility for the DEC 95 Call and DEC 95 Put are 19.2 and 22.4, respectively, then one can objectively state that IBM's implied volatility equals 20.8 ((19.2 + 22.4) / 2).

Trading Resource Guide

❖

Tools for Success in Options Trading

SUGGESTED READING LIST

MCMILLAN ON OPTIONS, ***Lawrence G. McMillan,*** Almost 600 pages from the world's leading expert on options gives a complete game plan for trading options. Here are McMillan's greatest strategies complete with precise instructions on how and when to use them. It's the definitive source for profitable option players.

570 PP $69.95 ITEM #T155X-2678

OPTIONS AS A STRATEGIC INVESTMENT, 3RD EDITION
Lawrence G. McMillan, It's the top selling options book of all time. Over 800 pages of exhaustive coverage on every aspect of trading options. Called "the single most important options reference available," this mammoth work teaches you to: track volatility and the key role it plays for traders; learn rules for entering/exiting trades at optimal levels, build a successful trading plan. Plus, must-read sections on LEAPS, CAPS, PERCS and cutting edge risk abatement techniques.

884 PP $49.95 ITEM #T155X-2836

THE OPTION ADVISOR, ***Bernie Schaeffer,*** This renowned options expert reveals the proven wealth-building techniques for selecting the right stocks, assessing risk, managing your options portfolio and—most importantly—for reading market timing indicators. In terms everyone can understand he provides solid ideas on how to use options effectively for conservative and aggressive traders.

316 PP $59.95 ITEM #T155X-5390

NEW OPTION SECRET–VOLATILITY, ***David Caplan,*** Uncovers practical strategies for using the most important variable in option pricing—volatility —to exploit and profit from the options market. Special section explains how "gurus" like Natenberg, Najarian, Trester and others use volatility to their benefit.

310 PP $65.00 ITEM #T155X-2889

To order any book listed and receive a special
15% "TRADE SECRETS" Discount
Call 1-800-272-2855 ext. T155

THE NEW OPTIONS ADVANTAGE, ***David Caplan*** **— Caplan presents proven strategies that can give you an edge in any market. Read about a no-loss, cost-free hedging method to protect profits, how to recognize and use under/over valued options, how to prevent the most common causes of loss.**

245 PP $45.00 ITEM #T155X-2861

OPTIONS FOR THE STOCK INVESTOR, ***James B. Bittman*** **— Explains how to use stock options safely and effectively, and how to integrate options into a long-term investment program. Learn time-proven strategies that add value to any investor's portfolio and tactics for investors with varying risk tolerances and goals. Topics include: Basic option strategies, Understanding price behavior, selling options on the stocks you own and using options to achieve long-term goals.**

225PP $29.95 ITEM #T155X-2419

OPTION VOLATILITY AND PRICING STRATEGIES, ***Sheldon Natenberg*** — Updated new edition tells you how to identify mispriced options and construct volatility and "delta neutral" spreads used by the pros. Using a non-technical trading approach, he leads the reader into the real world of option trading and applies his well developed pricing and volatility theories into practical, tradable strategies.

392 PP $50.00 ITEM #T155X-3009

OPTIONS ESSENTIAL CONCEPTS & STRATEGIES, 2ND EDITION, ***Options Institute*** — Expert advice from the "mecca" of options education, the CBOE's Option Institute. Each chapter focuses on a different essential for trading options. Part 1 covers option basics - what they are, how they're priced, how to trade them and pick a strategy. Part 2 contains practical advice for building a trading system - plus when to buy, sell and time trades, and applying the right strategy to current market conditions. The final section, "Real Time Applications" shows how to apply specific indicators to real world case studies.

402 PP $55.00 ITEM #T155X-2892

To order any book listed and receive a special
15% "TRADE SECRETS" Discount
Call 1-800-272-2855 ext. T155

THE COMPLETE OPTION PLAYER, 3RD EDITION SAVE 50%

Ken Trester — Perfect for those get into this market with limited capital, minimal risk and the possibility of spectacular profits. Profitable strategies that exploit little known discrepancies in option pricing, and other cutting edge trading methods - at a great price.

432 PP ITEM #T155X-2882 ~~$29.95~~ NOW $15

DEMARK ON DAY TRADING OPTIONS: *Using Options to Cash in on the Day Trading Phenomenon, Tom De Mark* —
The first book to combine the excitement of day trading with the continuing and growing popularity of options trading - using DeMark's specially developed indicators and techniques. Discover DeMark's "option trading variable" - the missing link to trading options successfully. Plus, selection best options to day trade, commonly used day trading methods - and more.

358 PP $34.95 ITEM #T155X-10450

CONSERVATIVE INVESTOR'S GUIDE TO TRADING OPTIONS

Leroy Gross - Foreword by Larry McMillan — Lots of safe and profitable options strategies for conservative investors. Plus, a full section of aggressive strategies for those willing to take slightly bigger risks. With a new introduction by options guru Larry McMillan, you'll find safe, low risk options methods along with ways to use options as a hedging tool. A great buy.

200 PP $34.95 ITEM #T155X-10267

TRADING INDEX OPTIONS, *James B. Bittman* — Proven techniques - minus all the math! New Book/Disk combo features the basics of index options - including spreads, how to match strategies with forecasts, alternatives for losing positions, and the importance of price behavior and volatility. Software included provides mulitiple pricing and graphing options.

312 PP $34.95 ITEM #T155X-2300

GETTING STARTED IN OPTIONS, 3RD EDITION, *Michael Thomsett* — This newly updated primer "Demystifies options for the individual investor." Great reference source for pros, and a hands-on starting point for new traders.

291 PP $19.95 ITEM #T155X-5691

To order any book listed and receive a special
15% "TRADE SECRETS" Discount
Call 1-800-272-2855 ext. T155

IMPORTANT INTERNET SITES

TRADERS' LIBRARY BOOKSTORE – *www.traderslibrary.com*, the #1 source for trading and investment books, videos and related products.

ESSEX TRADING COMPANY – *www.essextrading.com*, for important option software products and much more.

CHICAGO BOARD OF OPTIONS EXCHANGE – *www.cboe.com*, daily market statistics with extensive archives and introduction to options.

CHICAGO MERCANTILE EXCHANGE – *www.cme.com*, market data, live quote services, headlines, etc.

OPTION STRATEGIST – *www.optionstrategist.com*, short-term stock and options trading site on the latest techniques and strategies for trading a variety of innovative options products. Free weekly commentary, quotes, volatility data and other tools.

OPPORTUNITIES IN OPTIONS – *www.oio.com*, full service financial services company. Specialists in futures and options.

OPTIONETICS/OPTION ANALYSIS – *www.optionetics.com*, market updates, most active gainers/losers, market analysis, Index Charts, research, CMS Bond Quotes, resources and market reports.

INVESTORS BUSINESS DAILY –
www.traderslibrary.com/traders/ibd.cgi,
review the latest business news online.

TORONTO STOCK EXCHANGE – *www.tse.com*, news services, regulatory changes, the latest publications, newly listed companies, and comments from industry representatives.

WALL STREET DIRECTORY – *www.wsdinc.com*, provides access to the best financial sources located throughout the Internet.

About the Author and Essex Trading Company, Ltd.

Jay Kaeppel is the Director of Research at Essex Trading Company, Ltd. and an active Commodity Trading Advisor (CTA). With over 12 years of futures trading and system development experience, his expertise as a system developer has been noted by Technical Analysis of Stocks and Commodities magazine, which has published several of his articles on such diverse topics as:

- A Winning Approach to Futures Trading *
- Stock market timing with interest rates
- Stock market timing with the Stock/Bond Yield Gap
- Stock market timing with long-term price momentum
- Bond mutual fund investing and bond market timing *
- Gold mutual fund investing and gold market timing *

Jay Kaeppel is the subject of an interview in the May 1997 issue of *Technical Analysis of Stocks and Commodities* magazine, discussing stock market timing, stock selection techniques, trading system development and futures and option trading.

"Formula Research," a national monthly trading system development advisory edited by Nelson Freeburg has acknowledged Jay Kaeppel's expertise as a trading systems developer by using two of his original systems as the foundation of their own stock market and gold fund trading systems.

**Copies of these articles are available on the Essex Trading Company website.*

Essex Trading Company, Ltd. has been a leading developer of trading software for futures and option traders since 1983. Essex Trading Group, a division of Essex Trading Company, Ltd. is registered with the National Futures Association as a Commodity Trading Advisor and has been managing money since 1995. The President of Essex Trading Company, Ltd. is David Wesolowicz, a veteran trader with over 9 years of experience as a floor trader on the Chicago Board Options Exchange and the Chicago Board of Trade. Mr. Wesolowicz has over 16 years experience as a developer of software for trading applications. Together, Wesolowicz and Kaeppel have developed several software programs, most notably the award-winning Futures Pro and Option Pro On-Line programs.

COMPANY INFORMATION:

Essex Trading Company, Ltd.
107 North Hale, Suite 206
Wheaton, IL 60187
Phone: 800-726-2140 ext. 155 or 630-682-5780 ext. 155
Fax: 630-682-8065
E-mail address: essextr@aol.com
Internet Website address: http://www.essextrading.com

FREE DEMO DISK
CALL TODAY!
800-272-2855
ext 155
BONUS: Get a $20 gift certificate to Traders' Library with your FREE Demo Disk

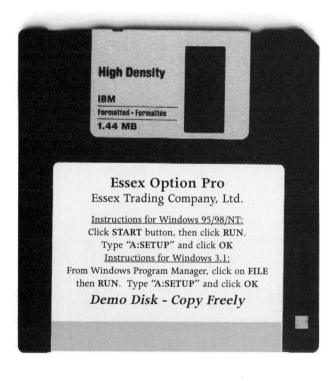